Greg,
May God bl-
you and keep you
Christ!   Jim
Matt 5:3
4/8/16

Only Surrender Remains

Jim Reynolds

WESTBOW
P R E S S®
A DIVISION OF THOMAS NELSON
& ZONDERVAN

Septuagint with Apocrypha: Greek and English
by Sir Lancelot C.L. Brenton.

Scripture taken from the King James Version of the Bible.

WestBow Press books may be ordered through
booksellers or by contacting:

WestBow Press
A Division of Thomas Nelson & Zondervan
1663 Liberty Drive
Bloomington, IN 47403
www.westbowpress.com
1 (866) 928-1240

ISBN: 978-1-5127-0527-0 (sc)
ISBN: 978-1-5127-0528-7 (e)

Library of Congress Control Number: 2015911945

Print information available on the last page.

WestBow Press rev. date: 07/27/2015

CONTENTS

"…That we should be holy and without blame before Him in love."

Ephesians 1:4

INTRODUCTION

I had to fight the temptation of adding more detail to this little book which I could have easily done, but that would have destroyed the simplicity achieved.

Lookie, we Christians make marriage too complicated. Believe me, from the pages of Scripture a wonderful marriage is openly and simply starring us in the face: that is, if we would only accept it. Please know, Scripture does not ask us to understand, only to accept: understanding will follow.

In Mark 8:14-21 the disciple's problem wasn't that they didn't understand. Their problem was they hadn't accepted Jesus for who he was despite the miracles. They, as with the Pharisees, wanted more proof and more proof: That is why they had purposefully forgotten to take bread with them in the ship except for that one loaf. They wanted Jesus to perform a mini miracle for their private viewing. For the most part, we are the same, "I'll accept what the Bible says once I understand it." Sorry, acceptance always comes before understanding; always. Again, I could go into scripture proof after proof and you would still not understand. Not until there is acceptance is there understanding. Here is the real issue: bold acceptance is risky. Knowing this, will you let the simplicity of this little book have its way into your heart?

One Scripture quote is from the (LXX): Sir Lancelot C. L. Brenton's translation of the <u>Septuagint with Apocrypha: Greek and English</u>; published by Regency Reference Library; Zondervan Publishing House; Grand Rapids, Michigan; 1851/1986. All other Scripture quotes are from the <u>King James Version</u>.

CHAPTER ONE

STRANGER AND PILGRIM

*And Job spake, and said, let the day
parish wherein I was born...*

Job 3:2, 3

I too cursed the day I was born. Like Job, I was not complaining. I simply hurt so much this was the only way I knew how to express my pain. The loneliness was so deep no other words could express the loss of my wife Pat.

At times alone, I would scream at God to kill me now, this minute. I don't want to live any longer.

The Lord knew how I felt, and as with Job, the Lord understood my cries.

The years alone without Pat have been the hardest years of my life, yet the best years: For it takes one of sorrows to know another of sorrows.

The Lord wrapped Himself around me as a cast would be to a broken leg, yet He did not take the pain away. My prayer life was that of continuous silent prayer. Words were not necessary. Nor did I need to form sentences in prayer. My life was now His life and He was mine.

Oh, as I went about my daily tasks; on the outside I was as normal as ever; yet inside, it was He and I in continuous union.

After three and half years, the Lord whispered that He was withdrawing His presence from me: taking off the cast. The time for healing was over. Nevertheless, there would remain a scar on my soul into eternity.

He also told me to take off my wedding ring. I was to now face the reality of my loneliness as a "stranger and pilgrim in this world" (1 Peter 2:11).

If marriage to Pat hadn't been so wonderful the pain of loneliness would not be so great now. She was such a joy to me. We were so very close. Even when separated we were together. Pat being who she was made me better than who I was, and my being who I was made Pat better than who she was: Truly, we were one flesh.

At times I still scream to God how lonely I am. Then I remember how lonely He was that day at Calvary... I sought His forgiveness. No matter how lonely I am His pain was so much greater than mine when He heard that cry from the cross: "My God, my God why hast thou forsaken me?" (Matt. 27:46)

CHAPTER TWO

ZIP YOUR LIP, DUCK, AND PRAY

As Pat's husband my job was to bring her, "holy and without blame before Him in love...with the washing of water by the word" (Eph. 1:4; 5:26). Likewise, Pat through her love and devotion for me secretly and silently was bringing me before the Lord, "holy and without blame" as well.

Marriage is the hardest thing I ever did. It is a job, a task, a responsibility and requires energy; lots of energy in the form of determination, knowledge, insight, confidence, honesty, honor, gentleness and humility. This is love.

The wife, through submission and respect, is to simply receive what the man gives.

I remember that first night when Pat gave me what the maiden gave the shepherd in the *(Song of Solomon 7:12; LXX)* *"Let us go early into the vineyards; let us see if the vine has flowered, if the blossoms have appeared, if the pomegranates have blossomed; there will I give thee my beasts"*: not as in a sexual act, but as an act of surrender. From that moment on only total surrender existed between Pat and me. From that first night to the very end Pat would not one time withhold herself from me. What a pleasant burden I must bear. How I must tenderly mold and shape this delicate soul that has placed all her trust in me. I must never betray that trust. That night she had placed the marriage into my hands.

Let me give you an example: Whenever I erred in dealing with Pat she would not retaliate; nor would she seek to change me. She would simply go silent in prayer and duck: not literally, but spiritually. She knew as long as she stood between me and the Lord that the Lord would not intervene. So, Pat learned early to simply "duck". When she did this it left me wide open to the Lord's rebuke. She never sought to change me. She left that up to the Lord.

It didn't take me long to keep a sharp eye on Pat to see if she was starting to "duck". I would take notice and quickly reevaluate my present attitude and actions before the Lord could respond to Pat's getting out of the way.

In counseling other ladies, Pat's favorite advice to them was, "Zip your lip, duck, and pray. God will straighten out your husband. As long as you are in the way God will not intervene in your marriage. Get out of the way and watch God work."

CHAPTER THREE

TIME FOR GOATS

Yes, the responsibility of the marriage is upon the husband. The wife can make his job easier or harder. Nevertheless, the job is his. He is to be the last to bed and the first to rise. However, more than physical responsibility is the spiritual. He must be a man of the Word, for it is the Word that gives the man his authority and respect with the wife. In fact, she craves this authority. All women want and need a man, but more than a man: they want a Godly man.

I realized my deficiency in the word and took inventory as for the reason why. I noticed when I did get up early enough to the reading of my Bible I kept falling asleep in the process (Much of the time I simply shut the alarm off never getting up to read).

So, I went and bought two milk goats and situated them outside our bedroom window. At the first sound from Lucy and Mamie I knew I must go quickly and milk them (There is no shutting up a milk goat when they need milking). By the time I finished milking, straining and refrigerating the milk I was as wide awake as could be.

The Word is alive and spirit breathed and after a few years of seriously taking the Word in a man can't help but be more Christ like: not so much in goodness, but in strength, spiritual strength. I still had my goof-ups and errors in judgment now and then, but a man immersed in the Word has the authority of that Word in him. Pat knew this and appreciated it openly. Oh, how she appreciated it! She was secure. She was secure physically and secure spiritually. She was now free to be the person God intended her to be for she now had a man of prayer covering her in the spiritual realm as well as the physical realm. This is peace found through unity: unity of two bodies, souls and spirits.

CHAPTER FOUR

GETTING IT IN ORDER

In high school Pat rode a motorcycle to school, an Indian. Not only did she fearlessly ride that machine, she could take it apart and put it back together again and again. She was a natural.

This was embarrassing to me for I was a total klutz when it came to auto mechanics.

We would be driving and Pat would say, "The left rear motor mount is loose. We need to get it fixed soon."

"Is it serious", I asked?

"Not immediately, but left unattended it could become serious."

Nevertheless, I kept putting it off until finally Pat took it into the shop. The men laughed to themselves that a woman would know such a thing. So Pat would chide them into putting the car on the lift. Giggling, they looked and sure enough not only was there a motor mount loose, it was the very one Pat said it was.

Over the years Pat's reputation spread until every mechanic in town would stand tall as Pat would go by as if she were some sort of mechanic goddess. It didn't hurt that Pat was an absolute stunner. She didn't seek the fame, it just happened.

This was not a good thing. "So Jim", I told myself: "You are going to have to learn to do the mechanics yourself. If I can't fix the car it will be me that takes the car to the shop, not Pat."

Oh, it had been easier just to let Pat handle the car problems. This fixed the car, but not our marriage.

There is an order to marriage and ours was slowly coming out of alignment. So, I asked Pat to put up her mechanics suit. I would handle the car problems from now on.

She went inside; took her mechanics suit; folded it up and tucked it away never to use it again. She understood the importance of marriage over a nice running car.

Oh, her continued mechanics wouldn't have ruined our marriage: at least not right away, but the marriage being out of order in this area is as a car with one motor mount loose. If left unattended it would certainly become serious down the road sometime.

CHAPTER FIVE

THEN ALONG CAME JAMES

The winter was cold and there was little work to be found except for the building of the new sewer treatment plant just down the road. As it would be, Pat was hired as the secretary to the out of state contractor. She worked in the supervisor's trailer, nice and warm.

As you would expect, Pat was more than a secretary. She was the girl Friday for the company. She knew all the key guys at the supply store and lumber yard. Pat somehow knew the manager at the cement plant. To the pleasure of the superintendent, Pat coordinated much of the concrete deliveries and supply needs. She knew the difference between double headed twenty penny and standard twenty penny nails: that a typical concrete truck could carry nine yards of concrete: and it was always to be 3/4 inch C grade sheets of plywood. When they said order more rebarb and catheads, she didn't have to ask what those are.

Pat got the super to hire me as a carpenter even though I knew nothing about carpentry. Because I was Pat's husband the supervisor didn't ever complain. He wanted to keep Pat happy. She was that valuable. I lasted the winter, and by the time spring came around I was pretty good at my new profession. Then along came James.

He was just a few months away from retirement and the supervisor assigned James to me, and at the same time gave us some of the lighter jobs to do. Guess the super had a tender spot for the old man.

One thing wrong with James: He was a heavy weekend drinker; the hard stuff, moonshine. However, he didn't touch the stuff during the work week. On Mondays James was useless. I had to do two men's work that day. Tuesday, James could at least use his hammer; that is if he didn't have to strike with much effort. On those days, I wouldn't let him get close to any of the electrical saws. Wednesday he was almost human, and Thursday and Friday he could turn out the work.

Next Monday it was the same thing and one Monday James arrived to the site with his bed room slippers. Oops, he quickly hopped back into the cab (He always rode a cab to work. The driver was a kin or something like that); went home; changed and finally snuck back in unnoticed. In the meantime I covered for him. Just another six weeks or so and he could retire.

The foreman did not like James. He simply didn't turn out the work. However, the foreman couldn't say anything because the superintendent liked James, as we all did.

Then one Monday when the super was in town for the day the foreman came up to the two of us; pulled James aside, and took him over to a large manhole structure that had been poured a few weeks earlier. It was time to strip the frames off the inside of the eight foot square and ten foot deep structure.

The foreman told James he had one hour to strip those forms or else he was fired. He lowered James into the pit and took off to the superintendent's trailer to have his coffee.

I waited ten minutes or so, and not seeing any action where James was; I looked around to see if the foreman was watching then went over, looked down into the pit and there was James just sitting there dejected. "Hey James, you only have forty five minutes and the foreman will be back."

"It don't matter, I can't do this. No need to try."

I said: "Get over in the corner. I'll help you." Away I went into stripping the forms, but I needed help. Just then two other guys came over and between the three of us we finished with minutes to spare.

We hurried back to our assigned jobs and sure enough here came the foreman right on time with coffee cup in hand. He quickly peered over the edge to try and surprise James. He was the one surprised. Just then James slung the last two by four wising by the foreman's head causing the foreman to spill his coffee. James yelled: "Help me out of here. I've got work to do." We all grinned.

James made it through the summer and retired. A month or so later James came over to our house with several steaks in hand with all the fixings. He said, "I told you I would cook you a steak dinner if you saw me through. Well, here I am."

Those were the best grilled steaks I ever ate, bar none.

CHAPTER SIX

JIM, YOU OK?

Not long after, the supervisor called all fifteen of the crew together telling how urgent this next project was. We had to have it finished and ready to pour before we could go home. Each man was given their specific task and off we went.

My job was to clear an area off to the side at the bottom of this crater like pit and frame in a four by four platform next to a larger site the other carpenters were to frame in (all down in this huge hole with sloping embankment all around).

The first thing I had to do was clear my site from small rocks. I threw the rocks into a small pile up behind me and left the largest rock for last (Was more a small boulder than a large rock). It was hot and I had a bandana tied around my forehead and cut off sleeves for a tee shirt. I was a stout six foot three with a full beard.

As I reached down to pick up that last rock and had it in my two hands ready to rise up, turn and toss it into the rock pile when unknown to me the foreman had made his way down to that small rock pile and shouted out for all to hear some awful things about Pat: I mean awful.

I froze, and so did all the other guys. Still bent down holding that large rock, I thought to myself: "I can't just let this go…what will all the guys think? What will Pat think? He had just insulted Pat in the worst way. Her honor is at stake…but I am a Christian and I must forgive him. I'll turn and toss this rock on the pile and then forgive him."

I stood up, with that rock in both hands raised high above my head and as I turned around, low and behold the foreman was squatted right there on that rock pile beneath me. I was towering over him.

"What do I do now?" I thought. However, before I could say anything the foreman in wide eyed fear stuttered out a lengthy apology. Quickly, he rose up and hurriedly climbed up the embankment and left.

I gingerly flip-tossed the rock right where he had been and went up the embankment to measure and cut the footer I was assigned to do.

As I measured the two by fours, I noticed none of the others had moved. They were all huddled to the side together discussing something among themselves. Little did I know, they had all thought I was going to crush the foreman's skull with that rock, and they were concerned it would be dangerous to say the wrong thing to me? No telling what I might do.

They appointed the one man that knew me the best, which wasn't much. After all I was an outsider: not really one of them.

Finally, after much deliberation they sent Glen over to see how I was (Everybody liked Glen. He had such a great sense of humor). He walked cautiously over to me and still keeping his distance whispered, "Jim, you OK?"

"Yep, I'm OK."

Satisfied, he turned and yelled back to all the others, "He's OK, get back to work."

From that time on I was some sort of hero among the crew as a man of honor (reluctantly, yet honor never the less). More than that, however, I now had a witness among this rough bunch of men. Little by little, one on one the men would approach me with their family problems. They could now trust me. I was one of them.

One man came to me when we could be alone and asked, "Jim, how can I tell my kid not to be a carpenter? He wants to be a carpenter like me. This is no work for any man. It's so hard and never steady."

I replied, "Somebody has to do it. Teach him to be the best carpenter ever."

The guy nodded and left with his head high. His son wanted to be just like his dad. That's a good thing.

CHAPTER SEVEN

PAT THE MIDWIFE

We were just finishing up the roof of the log cabin Pat, the boys and I built from scratch. I was on the roof finishing up shingling. Pat was below cutting the final shingles for the roof crown when a van drove up and out came a very pregnant woman and a perplexed looking man totally absorbed in his watch counting the minutes between contractions. We had never seen these two before, but it was certain this was a husband and wife about to have a baby.

The woman said to Pat, "Will you deliver my baby? It is due any time now. We were told you could do it."

Pat unfazed said, "I have never delivered a baby before, why not go to a doctor or hospital?"

"I don't like doctors, or hospitals. If you don't deliver this baby, my husband will. He has everything set up and ready, but I need you to do the delivery."

Pat looked at the husband then looked to me for approval then said, "Where do you live?"

We knew of the place, but never been there. This was a highly educated couple that lived over a swinging walk bridge in a primitive cabin tucked away in a beautiful cove. She taught at the local school, and some of the teachers had suggested Pat over her husband.

The husband had bought a book on how to deliver a baby and knew it from cover to cover. He had all the needed items for a proper home delivery. Yet, his lack of confidence betrayed him.

Pat issued one condition: "Tomorrow you must take the baby to the pediatrician to have it checked out, OK."

They agreed and with watch in hand off they went to their cabin to get ready.

Few minutes later after making a phone call to a friend, who Pat knew would be of help, Pat left. The two gals arrived at the swinging bridge; made their way over the river; and to the cabin where mother and father to be were waiting.

The delivery went smoothly, and the baby was a perfect little girl. By the time Pat arrived back I had finished the roof work and had the evening meal all ready. The pediatrician made sure all was well and that all the proper paper work was done. He added, "Any baby Pat delivered he would treat for free."

CHAPTER EIGHT

ALL IN A DAY'S WORK

Pat and I were outside working when the first phone call came to alert all the volunteer firefighters to a fire. Later while getting something inside the cabin the phone rang. I picked it up: "Jim there is a brush fire up Burnett Cove and nobody brought the four wheel drive water truck. Could you go by and get it?"

"Sure, I'm on my way."

Out there in the mountains, that was our fire alert system. Someone would call all the fire fighters of which I was a charter member:

CRUSO N.C.
NINE MILES OF FRIENDLY PEOPLE
PLUS ONE OLD CRAB

Most everyone suspected Marshall Cooper to be the "one old crab", but it was never confirmed.

The vehicle they wanted me to get was a modified four wheel drive jeep/truck that was fitted with a fifteen hundred gallon water tank and designed to negotiate narrow logging trails to access brush fires. Not knowing it was a brush fire the other guys only took the regular fire truck.

So, it was a good thing I missed the first phone call, because Burnett Cove was at the far end of our district.

Upon crossing the Burnett Cove Bridge I could see all the fire fighters high up a hill where the timber line met a farmer's pasture. I knew of the fire lane that came out where all the guys were gathered.

By the time I reached all the excitement, the guys told me they had put out the fire already and won't need me after all.

"OK, I'll just back it out of here."

Mengus, one of the leaders, said, "Nah, too far to back; just turn it around and go out front ways."

I looked down the hill. It was mighty steep and lead to a farm house at the bottom of this long pasture. If that vehicle decided to slide there was no stopping until it reached bottom: that is if it didn't flip first, and with all that water in the tank, flipping was a sure thing.

"Are you sure? I can back it out all right."

"Too far to back... I'll direct you."

So, I slowly began to turn there at the top of the pasture hoping to keep the water in the tank from shifting too much. I was to the place where I could pull forward when it happened: the water shifted tilting the truck onto the two driver side wheels with the two uphill wheels high in the air. I was on two wheels at a forty five degree angle looking straight down to the farm house below. I slammed hard on the break, and held the clutch in so there would be no movement.

Here I am one foot on the break, the other pushing the clutch in, both hands firmly gripping the steering wheel, the engine running and nobody knowing what to do. Some of the guys went to the down hill side in an attempt to keep the vehicle from tipping further, but some shouted out, "If that thing tips you'll all be crushed." So they went around where the two wheels were air born. Still no one knew what to do. My legs were beginning to cramp, especially the right leg holding down the break. The left leg wasn't far behind.

I surveyed the situation to myself: "If this thing tips over, I'll just have to ride it out. Can't jump or do anything. There would be no time, what happens, happens. OK Lord, if this is the way you want me to go then so be it."

Then someone said, "Hey, use the winch. There is a tree right up here. We can pull the vehicle up."

But no one moved. Who would reach in and manipulate the leavers to the winch. I couldn't move: had to keep my feet pressed hard on the break, and clutch. One tinny move and this thing is on its way down the mountain.

I don't know how long I was in this spot, but finally Art Huber said, "I'll do it."

Two guys held onto his belt as he reached in from the passenger side to maneuver the leavers to the winch. His feet dangling above the ground and from his waist up he was inside the cab with me.

It worked. With the cable around the tree and as the winch engaged, the truck settled calmly onto all four wheels and the vehicle was soon at the logging road, and I was off to the fire station. I put up the truck in it's spot, went home. I didn't ever mention the event. Why should I. If God wanted to take me then and there He would have done so. If not, then I would have survived even if the vehicle had flipped all the way down the mountain. It wasn't my call. It was His, but I was so glad Art did what he did. My cramped legs wouldn't have lasted much longer, and by the time I arrived back home, Pat had finished up outside and had the evening meal ready. "How did it go, Jim?"

"Just a brush fire: The guys had it out by the time I got there."

For me, it was all in a days work.

CHAPTER NINE

LOVE IS STRONG AS DEATH

After five years on the river in our log cabin, both Pat and I, on the same day, separately received notice from the Lord that we were to say good by to this beautiful place nestled in the shadows of the Shinning Rock Wilderness. We did not know when or where we were to go. So, once a day, each day, we said good by to this life the Lord had given us.

One year later almost to the day Pat received a phone call from her dad in Florida. He was going blind. Within two weeks we left taking only what we could haul in and on top of the car, leaving everything else behind with our neighbor.

It didn't take Pat long to figure out the problem with her dad. He was on so many different meds from so many different doctors that his system was being poisoned. Pat then found a great doctor she knew from years earlier, and between the two of them Pat's dad rebounded to live many years with full eyesight.

From Florida it was off to Texas, then to Minnesota, then back to Florida. Pat never complained. We moved again and again; all in the same way: We just gave stuff away and went with what we could carry in our car and by this time a small trailer. Pat never complained.

Finally, Pat and I were asking, "Lord, where to next": when our son called saying, "I am building a new house and thinking of putting a grandma and grandpa suite on it. Would you come?"

Off we went to our final destination, Cincinnati. Not once in forty eight years of marriage did Pat ever complain; not once. In fact, she could care less where we lived or how we lived. We never had much, but money just didn't matter to her. Our being together was everything. We were truly one.

Then the end was near. Pat's health was fading. She knew it. I knew it. Then two weeks before she was to go home, she told a friend, "My body chemistry has changed. Don't tell Jim": But, I sensed it anyway.

One by one Pat called to say good by to those she had known through the years. Please understand, those she called had no idea this was a good by call. Pat talked as if she only wanted to say hi and pass the time of day with them. Nevertheless, it was her way of saying good by.

Then three days before the end would come, Pat walked me into the bedroom. She sat at the head of the bed, "Get all my clothes and put them here."

I cleared out her closet and dresser, pilling everything high on the bed. Then one by one she had me put each item back in it's place with specific instructions for each:

"That goes to Kim. She has always liked that outfit."

"Reanata gets both of those."

"Marilyn is to have these three pair of shoes. I saw how she needs shoes especially now it is so cold, and I noticed she is my size. So they will fit nicely."

Finally, "What is left over or doesn't fit goes to Martha. She will know who should get what."

You see, Pat and I attended this small church in the inner city that ministered to drug addicts. There was both a men's home and women's home connected with the church. These restored drug addicts eat, sleep and live church. There is church Mondays, Thursdays evenings, and Saturday mornings; Tuesday is fast day; with women's Bible study Wednesday evenings, and men's Bible study Saturday evenings, and of course a three hour spirited Sunday morning worship service with a talented worship team, special music, and strong preaching. Most of all, everyone begins each morning with an hour of prayer. Then they go two by two into the streets witnessing to drug addicts. The church lives off of donations only, and each member is trained to start another church in yet another city. When they do go into a new city they seek out the very worst part of the city to plant that church as was this one in Cincinnati.

The gals loved Pat and treated her as the queen she was. In addition to Sundays, Pat would go to the women's Bible study Wednesday evenings. Pat had no fear: never did. Whenever Pat arrived at the women's home there were those that would sit on Pat's lap and just hug her as a child would their mother. However, Pat could scold them just as easily and they knew it. She was the mother they never had.

It was Sunday at midnight when Pat awoke to use the bathroom. I turned the light on as I always did and waited for her return. She came back saying, "Jim, I have a headache and it hurts so bad."

"OK, I'll get you something for it."

As I brought her the medicine, she sat on the bed; then laid her head back on the pillow and her "life left this earth" (Acts 8:33).

It was Monday, January 10, 2011. I was alone.

One week after the funeral I took all her clothes to the church and distributed them as instructed: Only surrender remains.

For love is strong as death.

Song of Solomon 8:6

EPILOGUE

I wrote this little book as simply as possible so the essence of marriage would be easily seen. Yet, more needs to be said. Therefore, I am adding this overview to help the reader get a better grip on Christian marriage. However, the first thing we need to ask is: What is marriage?

Marriage, a true Christian marriage, is the outward physical manifestation of the Gospel itself. The primary purpose of marriage is not to have children, but the purpose of marriage is to glorify God! Yes, children are important, but they are not the primary reason for marriage. Let me explain: The whole reason we are saved is to bring us: "...holy and without blame before him in love" (Eph. 1:4). My full motivation in our marriage was to bring Pat holy and without blame before the Lord in love. Knowingly or unknowingly Pat through her response to me was bringing me holy and without blame before him in love as well. Our children were and are secondary. You build a strong marriage, and the children will follow.

Marriage is a union, thus one flesh. This physical union is a pattern of our individual spiritual union with the Father. Being close to Pat brought me that much closer to the Lord. But union takes work, lots of work.

For the man, marriage is the hardest thing he will ever do (Men, I cannot emphasize just how much energy must be employed into the marriage). A good marriage just doesn't come to you. The man must supply the energy to the marriage for it to prosper. He brings his strength to the woman. She then receives that strength. This is vividly demonstrated in the marital sex act (Yes men, you are the initiator of sex in marriage. The wife can make your efforts harder or easier. Pat made mine easy; oh, how wonderfully easy).

Not only is the man to bring physical strength to the marriage, he is to bring the spiritual strength as well. Again, the wife can make his task easier or harder. Pat made mine easy.

Yes ladies, so often the husband is a klutz when it comes to his being the husband he is meant to be. Nevertheless, you cannot change him. This will only glom up the works. It is God and God alone that changes the husband, and as long as you are in the way God will not intervene. Like Pat, you women must learn to "Zip your lip, duck and pray". Then watch God work. Be careful, dear ladies, you may in fact be the one that is in need of change.

The husband, besides being the provider and security to the wife, must be above all a man of the Word. For it is the Word that gives the man the authority in the marriage: little Word, little to no authority. Trying to exercise authority absent of the Word only brings stress and anxiety to the marriage. Right here is where I get confused looks from the men. The reason being, so few men are into the Word, and the connection between authority and the Word is foreign to them.

Not until I took Bible study seriously did our marriage begin to jell. For me, it took two milk goats before I came to seriously and methodically study the Bible two to four hours a day. Men, if you can't raise goats you must do something to secure serious Bible study for yourselves: ten times out of ten that means having to do something about that TV.

In today's world many women will recoil to Pat's having put up her mechanics suit, however Pat knew God had established an order to marriage. Just as there is an order in Christ's relationship to the church, there is the same relationship of the husband to the wife in marriage. Christ is the doer, the church is to be. Likewise, the husband is the doer and the wife is to be.

Thus, the wife is the reflection of the husband: not the other way around.

Likewise, ye husbands, dwell with
them according to knowledge,
giving honour unto the wife, as unto
the weaker vessel, and as being
heirs together of the grace of life; that
your prayers be not hindered.
1Peter 3:7

Note, when the marriage is out of order it is the husband's prayers that are hindered, not the wife's.

Why is this? In creating man and women God built into the relationship an order. Let me explain:

And the Lord God formed man of the
dust of the ground, and breathed
into his nostrils the breath of life; and
the man became a living soul.
Genesis 2:7

Now, look at how Eve was created and note the difference.

And the Lord God caused a deep sleep
to fall upon Adam, and he slept:
and he took one of his ribs, and closed
up the flesh instead thereof; and
the rib, which the Lord God had taken
from the man, made he a
woman, and brought her to the man.
Genesis 2:21, 22

The man received his spirituality directly from God, and the woman received her spirituality from the man. Thus, the man is a reflection of the Lord and the woman is a reflection of the man. Can we see how the woman is the weaker vessel both physically and spiritually? Because of this, the woman is to be in subjection to the man (Eph. 5:22).

Ladies, you can fight this all you want, but you will never change the truth of the matter. It has been done and won't be undone. Will you accept this?

A girl is under the covering of her father until she gets married. As she comes down the isle on her wedding day with her father; the groom is waiting. The two stop when they come along side the waiting groom. The father then places his daughter's hand into the groom's hand. Then the young couple proceed to the alter leaving the father. The father did his job and the groom's job has just begun (Eph. 5:25-27).

This act though seemingly insignificant has paramount spiritual ramifications. From birth to her wedding, the daughter is covered both physically and spiritually by her father. As long as she is obedient to her father Satan has no rights in her life (I am talking of a Christian family). Only when she comes out from under his covering through disobedience can Satan touch her. Once she becomes obedient again, Satan is again bound by the father's covering.

By the father placing the daughter's hand into the hand of the groom's the girl's spiritual covering is being transferred to her husband (Again, we are dealing with a Christian marriage). Consequently, the spiritual covering is never broken. That exchange of hands does not go unnoticed in the spiritual realm and as long as the bride remains obedient to her husband Satan cannot touch her. This right here is why Pat put away her mechanics suit. By doing so she was getting back in order.

Girls, I want you to notice; while you are in obedience to your father or husband all of Satan's temptations to you are to lure you out from under your covering so you will then be free game for his demons. Think about it.

...and thy desire shall be to thy husband.
Genesis 3:16

Note how the foreman sought to drive a wedge between Pat and me. It didn't work. In fact, it backfired on him. Then, when approached by the couple having a baby Pat sought my approval before accepting, thus remaining in order and a perfect baby girl came into this world. Then a potential disaster on a steep slope came to naught. As hard as Satan might, he cannot penetrate a marriage in order and under the authority of the Word. On the contrary, all three of these events (and countless more) had God's fingerprints all over them.

This is a great mystery: but I speak
concerning Christ and the church.
Ephesians 5:32

The man is not superior nor is he of greater value than the wife. Both are of equal value before God, but there is an order, and a good Christian marriage is a witness to God's order and the Gospel of Jesus Christ.

The husband must be a man under authority of the Word to exercise authority in the marriage. The woman, through submission recognizes that authority until only surrender remains.

CPSIA information can be obtained
at www.ICGtesting.com
Printed in the USA
FFOW05n0157050815